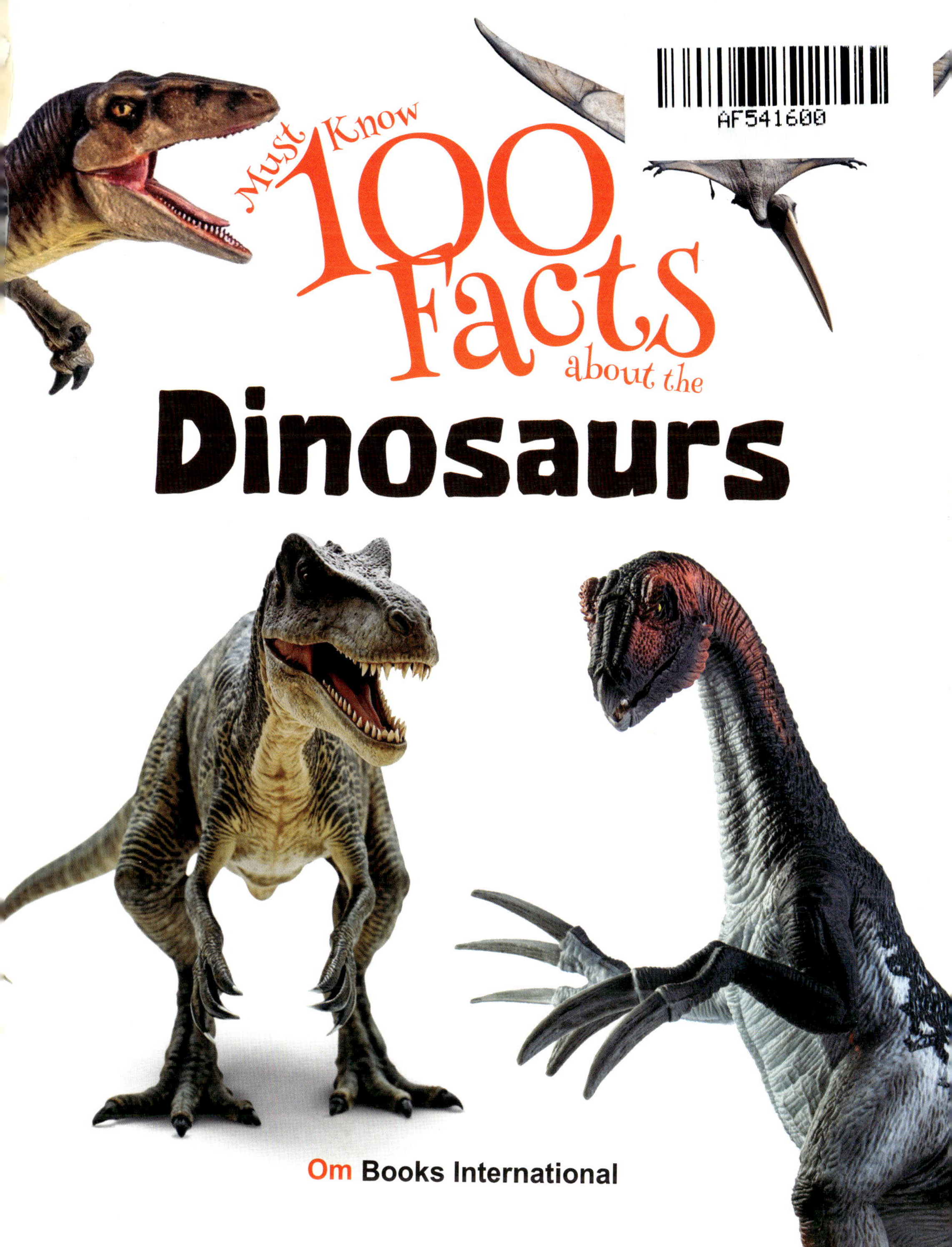
AF541600
Must Know
100
Facts
about the
Dinosaurs
Om Books International

First Published in 2025 by

Om Books International

Corporate & Editorial Office
A-12, Sector 64, Noida 201 301
Uttar Pradesh, India
Phone: +91 120 477 4100
Email: editorial@ombooks.com
Website: www.ombooksinternational.com

Sales Office
107, Ansari Road, Darya Ganj
New Delhi 110 002, India
Phone: +91 11 4000 9000
Email: sales@ombooks.com
Website: www.ombooks.com

ISBN: 978-93-52761-87-6

Printed in India

10 9 8 7 6 5 4 3 2 1

CONTENTS

DINOSAUR BASICS

Fun Fact

Dinosaur eggs used to come in all shapes and sizes, with some as big as a football and others no bigger than a tennis ball. That's a lot of different-sized omelettes!

WHAT'S IN A NAME?

The term 'dinosaur' was coined by Sir Richard Owen in 1842. In Greek, it means 'terrible lizard' though dinosaurs are not lizards.

THE THREE PERIODS

Dinosaurs lived during the Mesozoic Era, which is divided into three periods: Triassic, Jurassic, and Cretaceous.

DIVERSE DIETS

Dinosaurs were herbivores, carnivores, and omnivores. For example, the Stegosaurus was a herbivore, while the Tyrannosaurus rex was a carnivore.

GLOBAL INHABITANTS

Fossils show that dinosaurs lived on every continent on Earth, including Antarctica.

FEATHERS AND SCALES

Evidence suggests that many dinosaurs, including the fierce Velociraptor, had feathers along with their scales.

FAMOUS DINOSAURS

TYRANNOSAURUS REX

T.rex, one of the most well-known dinosaurs, had one of the strongest bites known in the animal kingdom.

TRICERATOPS

The Triceratops had between 400 and 800 teeth. They continuously grew new teeth throughout their life.

Fun Fact

The first dinosaur ever named was Megalosaurus, way back in 1824.

VELOCIRAPTOR

The real Velociraptor was actually the size of a turkey and not as depicted in the popular Jurassic Park movies.

BRACHIOSAURUS

Brachiosauruses were known for their long necks, which they may have used to reach high vegetation.

STEGOSAURUS

The Stegosaurus had a brain roughly the size of a walnut, making it one of the smallest relative to body size among dinosaurs.

EXTINCTION EVENTS

THE BIG ASTEROID

Around 66 million years ago, a massive asteroid hit what is now the Gulf of Mexico, causing the extinction of nearly 75% of Earth's species, including most dinosaurs.

VOLCANIC ACTIVITY

Massive volcanic eruptions created the Deccan Traps in India. It also played a role in the dinosaurs' extinction by altering the global climate.

Fun Fact

Shockwaves from the asteroid impact that wiped out the dinosaurs could have circled the Earth multiple times!

CLIMATE CHANGE

Dramatic climate changes before the asteroid impact had already begun stressing ecosystems, contributing to the decline of the dinosaurs.

SURVIVAL OF THE BIRDS

Birds are considered the only surviving dinosaurs, evolving from theropods. It is a subgroup of saurischian dinosaurs.

RISING MAMMALS

The extinction of dinosaurs gave mammals an opportunity to rise and diversify. They had lived in their shadows for millions of years.

BIOLOGY AND BEHAVIOUR

Fun Fact

Dinosaurs may have had seasonal colour changes in their skin, like chameleons, to blend into their environments.

HERDING BEHAVIOUR

Evidence from fossilised tracks suggests that some dinosaur species, like hadrosaurs, lived and migrated in large herds.

DINOSAUR GROWTH

Many dinosaurs, like the Apatosaurus, grew incredibly fast. They reached adult size in just a few years.

NESTING HABITS

Fossils of dinosaur eggs, nests, and even embryos provide evidence that many dinosaurs, such as the Oviraptor, cared for their young.

THERMOREGULATION

Some scientists believe dinosaurs were warm-blooded, like birds. This trait would explain their active lifestyles and widespread distribution.

COMMUNICATION

Dinosaurs used visual displays, sounds, and possibly even smells to communicate with one another.

RECORD-BREAKING DINOSAURS

Fun Fact

The Microraptor had four wings, one on each limb. It could glide between trees like a squirrel!

LARGEST CARNIVORE

The Spinosaurus is considered the largest carnivorous dinosaur. It measures over 50 feet long and weighs up to 7 tons.

HEAVIEST DINOSAUR

The Argentinosaurus is estimated to have weighed up to 100 tons. They measured up to 120 feet long, making it the heaviest dinosaurs.

LONGEST NECK

The Sauroposeidon had a neck that measured up to 39 feet long, one of the longest of any known dinosaur.

SMALLEST DINOSAUR

The Compsognathus, was about the size of a chicken, making it one of the smallest known dinosaurs.

THICKEST SKULL

The Pachycephalosaurus had a skull up to 10 inches thick. It was used potentially for head-butting during mating contests.

DINOSAUR HABITATS AND LOCATIONS

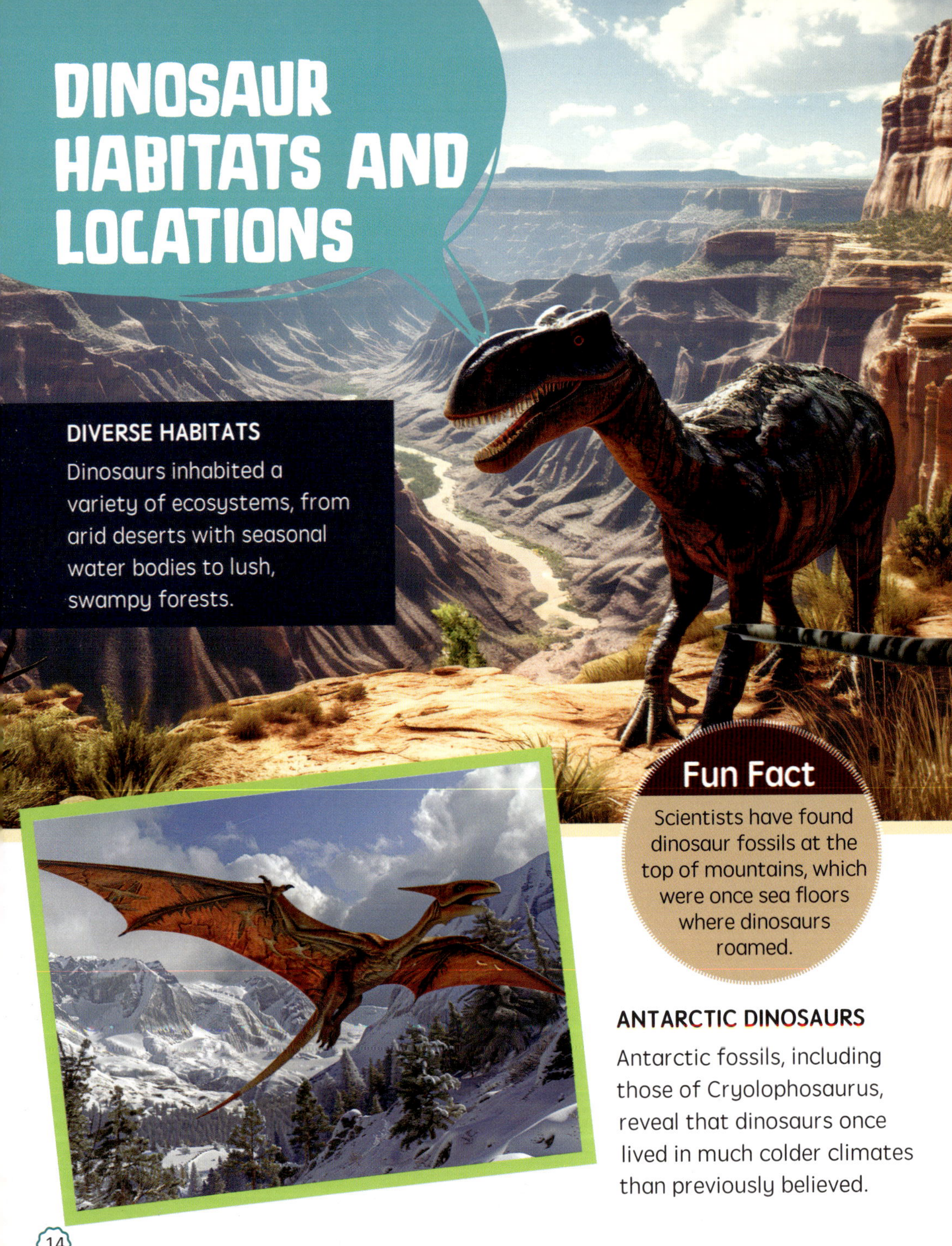

DIVERSE HABITATS

Dinosaurs inhabited a variety of ecosystems, from arid deserts with seasonal water bodies to lush, swampy forests.

Fun Fact

Scientists have found dinosaur fossils at the top of mountains, which were once sea floors where dinosaurs roamed.

ANTARCTIC DINOSAURS

Antarctic fossils, including those of Cryolophosaurus, reveal that dinosaurs once lived in much colder climates than previously believed.

DESERT DWELLERS

The Coelophysis is one of the oldest known dinosaur species. They thrived in the arid conditions of what is now the American Southwest.

AQUATIC ADAPTATIONS

No dinosaurs are known to have been fully aquatic. However, recent evidence suggests that some, like Spinosaurus, had adaptations for spending significant time in the water.

MOUNTAIN GIANTS

The Himalayas were still forming during the Cretaceous period. Footprints found at high altitudes suggest that some of the largest dinosaurs may have lived there.

DINOSAUR DISCOVERIES AND PALEONTOLOGY

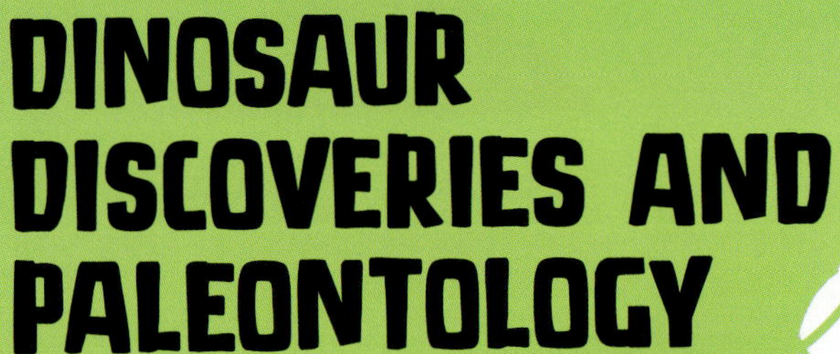

FIRST DINOSAUR FOSSILS

The first recognised dinosaur fossils were discovered in the early 19th century by Mary Anning in England. Though they were not initially recognised as dinosaurs!

Fun Fact

The smallest dinosaur footprint ever found is only about 1 cm wide, smaller than a penny!

BONE WARS

The 'Bone Wars' refers to the intense rivalry between palaeontologists Edward Drinker Cope and Othniel Charles Marsh, which led to the discovery of over 142 new species of dinosaurs.

MODERN PALEONTOLOGY

Today, techniques like CT scans and 3D modelling help palaeontologists study dinosaur fossils without damaging them.

FEATHERED FOSSILS

The discovery of feathered dinosaur fossils in China has provided crucial evidence. This discovery linked dinosaurs to modern birds.

DINOSAUR MUMMIES

Rare 'mummified' dinosaur fossils with preserved skin and soft tissues. These discoveries have offered unprecedented details about their appearance and biology.

THEORIES AND CONTROVERSIES

WARM-BLOODED VS. COLD-BLOODED

Scientists continue to debate whether dinosaurs were warm-blooded like mammals and birds, or cold-blooded like reptiles.

Fun Fact

Some experts believe that many dinosaurs were actually warm-blooded, much like mammals, not cold-blooded like reptiles.

COLOURATION THEORIES

Recent advances in fossil analysis suggest that some dinosaurs, such as the Microraptor, had iridescent feathers.

SOCIAL BEHAVIOUR

Debates persist about the social behaviour of dinosaurs, including whether tyrannosaurids were solitary hunters or social pack animals.

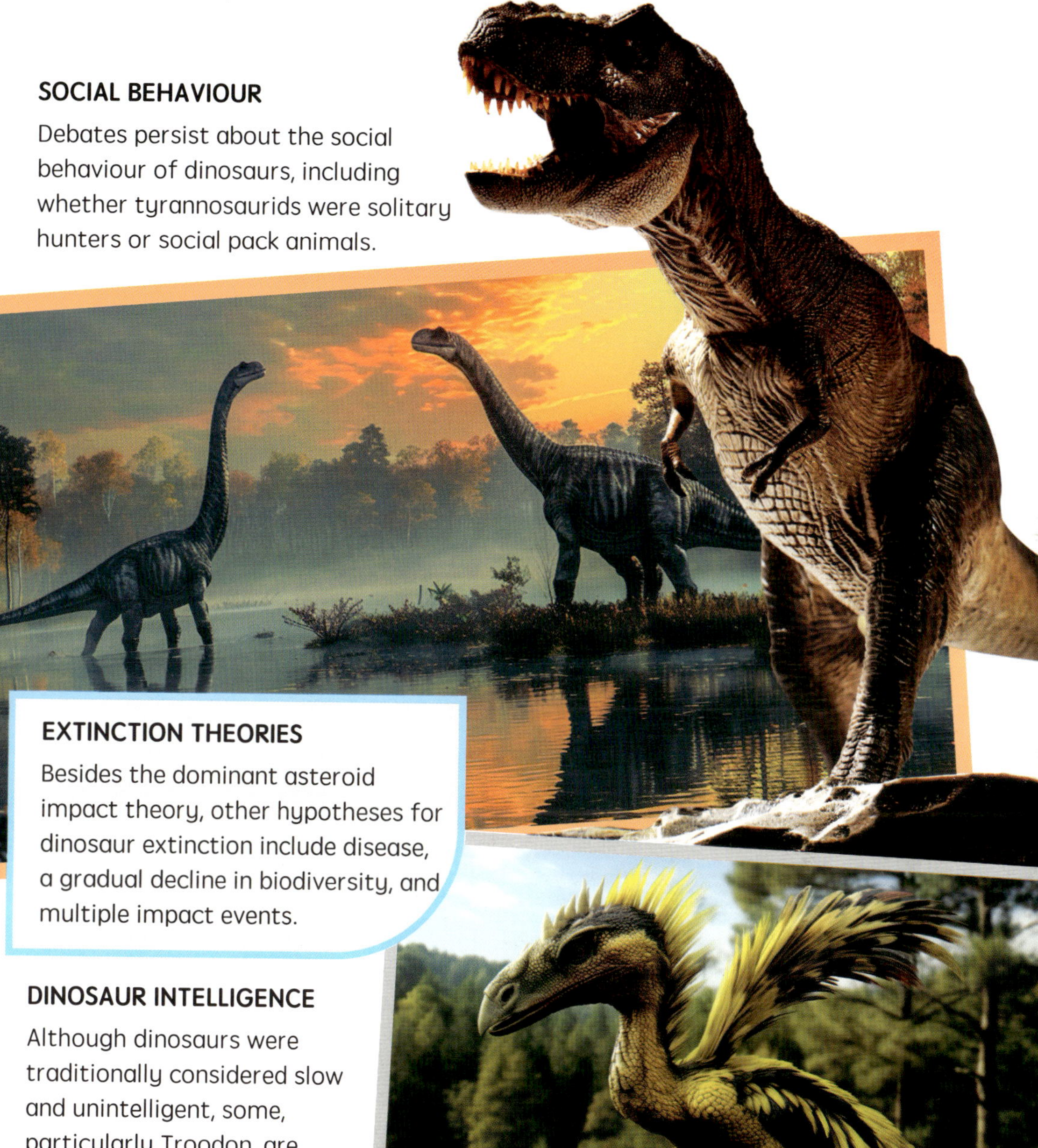

EXTINCTION THEORIES

Besides the dominant asteroid impact theory, other hypotheses for dinosaur extinction include disease, a gradual decline in biodiversity, and multiple impact events.

DINOSAUR INTELLIGENCE

Although dinosaurs were traditionally considered slow and unintelligent, some, particularly Troodon, are now thought to have had a relatively high brain-to-body mass ratio. This suggests they may have exhibited more complex behaviour.

DINOSAUR INFLUENCE IN CULTURE

CINEMA IMPACT

Dinosaurs have been a popular subject in cinema since the early 20th century, with films like Jurassic Park renewing widespread interest in dinosaurs.

Fun Fact

A dinosaur named Sue is the most complete T. rex skeleton ever found. She even has a Twitter account maintained by the museum where she resides!

LITERATURE AND LEGENDS

Myths and legends from various cultures may have been inspired by dinosaur fossils; for example, dragons in European and Asian folklore.

DINOSAUR MUSEUMS

Dinosaur museums around the world, such as the American Museum of Natural History in New York and the Natural History Museum in London, play crucial roles in public education.

DINOSAURS IN EDUCATION

Dinosaurs are a staple in educational programmes, engaging children in science from an early age.

COMMERCIAL USE

The imagery of dinosaurs has been widely used in marketing, from toys and video games to clothing and even technology.

NEW FRONTIERS IN DINOSAUR SCIENCE

GENETIC RESEARCH

Scientists are exploring the possibilities of recovering DNA from dinosaur fossils, though this remains a challenging and controversial field.

Fun Fact

Scientists are using laser technology to reveal hidden details in fossils that are invisible to the human eye.

SOFT TISSUE DISCOVERIES

Discoveries of soft tissue in certain dinosaur fossils have opened new research avenues into their biology and physiology.

BEHAVIOURAL STUDIES

Advanced simulation technologies allow scientists to study how dinosaurs might have moved and behaved, based on the structure of their skeletons.

PALEOECOLOGY

The study of ancient ecosystems offers insights into how dinosaurs interacted with their environment and other species.

DINOSAUR GROWTH RINGS

Like trees, some dinosaur bones have growth rings that can tell us about the life history and environmental conditions of these ancient creatures.

UNUSUAL DINOSAURS

DREADNOUGHTUS' MASSIVE SIZE

The Dreadnoughtus, discovered in Argentina, is one of the largest land animals that ever existed. They are estimated to weigh about 65 tons.

THERIZINOSAURUS' GIANT CLAWS

The Therizinosaurus is known for having the longest claws of any dinosaur. Each claw could measure up to three feet long.

Fun Fact

There was a dinosaur called Epidexipteryx that had bizarre, ribbon-like feathers, unlike any bird we see today.

SPINOSAURUS' AQUATIC LIFESTYLE

The Spinosaurus is the first dinosaur known to have been semi-aquatic. They are adapted to both swimming and walking on land.

PARASAUROLOPHUS' HEAD CREST

The Parasaurolophus had a long, backward-curving crest on its head. It likely functioned as a resonance chamber to create sounds.

AMARGASAURUS' NECK SPINES

The Amargasaurus featured two parallel rows of tall spines down its neck. They could have been used for display or thermoregulation.

DINOSAUR FOSSILS AND THEIR SECRETS

OLDEST DINOSAUR NEST

The oldest known dinosaur nesting site, found in South Africa, is about 190 million years old. It contains clutches of Massospondylus eggs.

TRACE FOSSILS

Beyond bones, trace fossils such as footprints, skin impressions, and coprolites (fossilised dung) provide rare insights into the daily lives of dinosaurs.

Fun Fact

The colour of some dinosaur feathers has been discovered through microscopic structures in fossils that survived millions of years!

FOSSILIZATION PROCESS

For a dinosaur bone to become fossilised, it must be rapidly buried by sediment. Over time minerals gradually replace the organic material.

GLOBAL DISTRIBUTION

Dinosaur fossils have been found on every continent, indicating they lived in a variety of environments and climates.

LARGEST DINOSAUR GRAVEYARD

The Cleveland-Lloyd Dinosaur Quarry in Utah is one of the largest concentrations of Jurassic dinosaur bones ever found.

DINOSAUR ANATOMY AND ADAPTATIONS

HOLLOW BONES

Many dinosaurs, like birds, had hollow bones. They helped to reduce the weight of their large bodies.

Fun Fact

Some dinosaurs had air sacs in their bones to make them lighter. They helped the larger species to move more easily.

TEETH REPLACEMENTS

Dinosaurs like Tyrannosaurus could replace their teeth. They lost them regularly due to wear and damage.

VISION

Many predatory dinosaurs, including the Velociraptor, had forward-facing eyes for depth perception. They were crucial for hunting.

GIZZARD STONES

Some herbivorous dinosaurs swallowed stones that stayed in their stomachs to help grind up tough plant material.

TAIL WEAPONS

Dinosaurs such as Ankylosaurus and Stegosaurus had tails modified into formidable weapons against predators.

DINOSAUR ECOLOGY

NICHE SPECIALIZATION

Dinosaurs exhibited a high degree of niche specialization. For example, some had beaks suited for cropping specific types of vegetation.

Fun Fact

Dinosaurs played a key role in the early distribution of flowering plants through their eating and digestive habits.

ROLE AS PREDATORS AND PREY

Large carnivores like Allosaurus played the role of apex predators. In contrast, large herbivores like Diplodocus were the primary consumers in their ecosystems.

IMPACT ON VEGETATION

Large herds of sauropods could have significantly altered the landscape. This is similar to modern elephants, trampling through dense forested areas.

SEASONAL BEHAVIOURS

Evidence suggests that some dinosaurs migrated seasonally to exploit different food sources and climates.

PREDATION AND DEFENSE

The arms race between predator and prey dinosaurs led to a variety of defensive adaptations, including armour, speed, and herding behaviours.

EVOLUTIONARY INSIGHTS

FROM DINOSAURS TO BIRDS

The evolutionary transition from theropod dinosaurs to birds is one of the most well-documented evolutionary transformations.

ADAPTIVE RADIATION

Following the Triassic-Jurassic mass extinction, dinosaurs underwent rapid adaptive radiation, filling ecological niches left by extinct competitors.

Fun Fact

The oldest known bird, Archaeopteryx, provides a crucial link between feathered dinosaurs and modern birds.

SURVIVAL STRATEGIES

Dinosaurs developed various survival strategies, including gigantism, miniaturisation, and armoured bodies. They developed these techniques to adapt to the Mesozoic environment.

METABOLIC RATES

Studies on growth rings in bones suggest that some dinosaurs had growth patterns similar to warm-blooded animals. This indicates higher metabolic rates than reptiles.

FEATHER EVOLUTION

Feathers evolved initially for insulation or display and only later became adapted for flight in birds.

DINOSAUR EXTREMES

SMALLEST EGGS

The smallest known dinosaur eggs are about the size of a chicken egg. They are likely laid by a small theropod.

Fun Fact

The largest meat-eating dinosaur discovered so far is Spinosaurus, which was even larger than T.rex!

LARGEST EGGS

The largest dinosaur eggs, found in China, belong to the Hypselosaurus. They measure up to 24 inches in length.

FASTEST DINOSAURS

The Ornithomimus could likely run up to 40 miles per hour, making it one of the fastest dinosaurs. They resemble the modern ostriches.

SLOWEST DINOSAURS

The massive Argentinosaurus, while being one of the largest dinosaurs, was also among the slowest, moving at speeds similar to a human's walking pace.

LONGEST CLAWS

Therizinosaurus had the longest claws of any known animal, measuring up to 3 feet long, used for foraging or defense.

DINOSAUR COMMUNICATION AND INTELLIGENCE

Fun Fact

Researchers believe some dinosaurs could produce a range of complex sounds to communicate.

GROUP LIVING

Social interactions are evident in species like Velociraptor, which may have hunted in packs, similar to wolves.

CALLS AND CRIES

Evidence suggests that dinosaurs, like the Parasaurolophus, used their crested heads to amplify calls. It is potentially done for communication across large distances.

PARENTAL CARE

Fossils of species like the Maiasaura indicate that they exhibited complex parental care, including feeding their young after hatching.

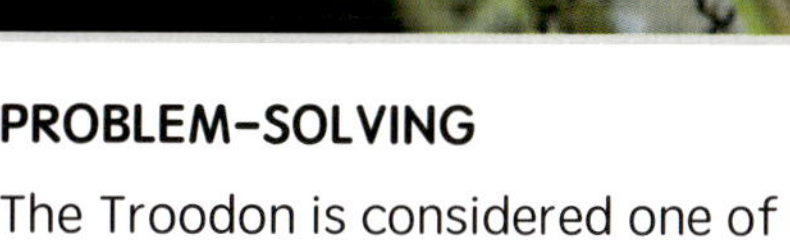

PROBLEM-SOLVING

The Troodon is considered one of the smartest dinosaurs due to its large brain relative to its body size. This ability may have enabled complex behaviours.

EMOTIONAL EXPRESSION

While hard to prove, some palaeontologists speculate that dinosaurs could have had the capacity for emotions and social bonding.

ICONIC DINOSAUR DISCOVERIES

Fun Fact

A dinosaur graveyard in Alberta, Canada, has yielded fossils of over 500 dinosaurs. This discovery provides incredible insights into their lives.

SUE THE T. REX

One of the most complete and best-preserved Tyrannosaurus rex specimens, named Sue, was found in South Dakota in 1990. It is displayed at the Field Museum in Chicago.

FIGHTING DINOSAURS

The famous 'Fighting Dinosaurs' fossil features a Velociraptor locked in combat with a Protoceratops. It vividly illustrates predator-prey interaction.

FEATHERED DISCOVERIES

The discovery of Sinosauropteryx in China in the 1990s provided groundbreaking evidence of the connection between birds and dinosaurs. This fossil showed clear evidence of feathers, supporting the link between the two groups.

THE FIRST AMERICAN DINOSAUR

The Hadrosaurus, the first dinosaur skeleton to be mounted, was discovered in 1858 in New Jersey. It proved that dinosaurs could be bipedal.

JURASSIC PARK INSPIRATION

The fossilised remains of a giant prehistoric mosquito inspired the fictional story of Jurassic Park. It was discovered in Montana.

DINOSAUR MYSTERIES AND UNANSWERED QUESTIONS

Fun Fact

Some palaeontologists theorise that dinosaurs may have danced as part of their mating rituals, similar to birds today.

COLOURATION MYSTERY

Scientists are still unsure about the full range of colours dinosaurs exhibited. Although pigment structures in some fossils suggest a variety of hues.

SLEEPING POSITIONS

How dinosaurs slept remains largely unknown. But some fossils show them curled up, similar to modern birds.

DINOSAUR LIFESPAN

Estimating the lifespans of dinosaurs is challenging. But some like the Tyrannosaurus rex might have lived up to 30 years.

DISEASE IN DINOSAURS

Fossil evidence shows signs of diseases like cancer and arthritis in dinosaurs. It offers a glimpse into their health challenges.

EXTINCTION SURVIVORS

How certain species survived the mass extinction that wiped out the dinosaurs, remains a key question in palaeontology.

REVIVING DINOSAURS: SCIENCE AND IMAGINATION

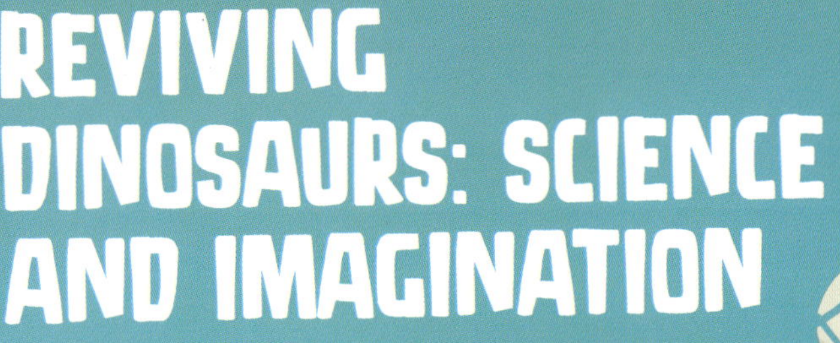

DE-EXTINCTION DEBATE

The scientific and ethical debate over potentially reviving dinosaurs or dinosaur-like creatures using genetic technologies continues to captivate imaginations.

Fun Fact

Geneticists are debating the ethics of possibly bringing back dinosaurs using DNA editing, sparking real-life Jurassic Park discussions!

CULTURAL FASCINATION

Dinosaurs continue to be a major part of popular culture. They inspire films, books, and exhibits that explore their might and mystery.

EDUCATIONAL ROLE

Dinosaurs play a crucial role in education. They help to engage students with natural history and scientific inquiry.

TECHNOLOGICAL ADVANCES

Advances in technology, such as AI and machine learning, are helping scientists unlock even more secrets from the fossil record.

FUTURE DISCOVERIES

New dinosaur species are discovered every year, suggesting that much about these ancient creatures remains to be uncovered.

DINOSAURS IN POLAR REGIONS

ANTARCTIC ANKYLOSAUR DISCOVERY

In 1986, fossils of Antarctopelta oliveroi, an ankylosaurian dinosaur, were unearthed on James Ross Island, Antarctica. This medium-sized herbivore, measuring approximately 4 metres in length, is the only known ankylosaur from the continent.

EARLY JURASSIC ANTARCTIC DINOSAURS

Glacialisaurus hammeri, a basal sauropodomorph, was discovered in the Hanson Formation of Antarctica. This dinosaur lived approximately 190 million years ago, suggesting that early Jurassic Antarctica had forests populated by a diverse range of species, at least along the coast.

ARCTIC DINOSAUR DISCOVERIES

Fossils of various dinosaur species, including theropods, ankylosaurs, and hadrosaurs, have been discovered along Alaska's North Slope. These findings indicate that dinosaurs inhabited polar regions during the Cretaceous period.

ADAPTATIONS TO POLAR LIGHT CONDITIONS

During winter months, dinosaurs in polar regions lived through extended periods of darkness. Their ability to survive in such environments suggests possible adaptations to limited light availability.

POLAR DINOSAUR MIGRATION THEORIES

Some scientists propose that certain polar dinosaurs, such as hadrosaurids, may have migrated to warmer regions as winter approached. However, the energy required for such migrations suggests that many polar dinosaurs were likely warm-blooded and capable of enduring colder climates.

PALAEONTOLOGICAL INSIGHTS FROM POLAR DINOSAURS

PRESERVATION OF POLAR DINOSAUR FOSSILS

The discovery of dinosaur fossils in polar regions has provided unique insights into their anatomy and behaviour. For instance, the Antarctopelta specimen includes various bones and numerous pieces of armour, offering valuable information about its physical characteristics.

DIVERSE POLAR DINOSAUR FAUNA

The Snow Hill Island Formation in Antarctica has yielded fossils of various dinosaur species, including ornithopods like Trinisaura. This diversity suggests that polar regions supported a variety of dinosaur species.

INSIGHTS INTO DINOSAUR BEHAVIOUR

The presence of dinosaurs in polar regions provides clues about their behaviour and physiology. For example, the discovery of nesting sites at high latitudes suggests that some dinosaurs were capable of reproducing in these extreme environments.

CLIMATE IMPLICATIONS

The presence of dinosaurs in Mesozoic polar regions suggests these areas possessed climates significantly warmer than today, supporting diverse ecosystems.This challenges previous assumptions about ancient climate patterns.

EVOLUTIONARY SIGNIFICANCE

Studying polar dinosaurs helps palaeontologists understand how these animals adapted to extreme environments, shedding light on their evolutionary processes and resilience.

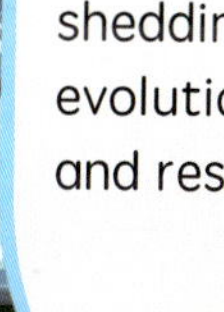

Titles in this Series

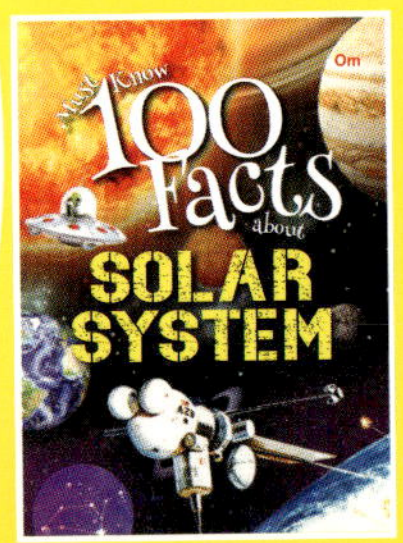

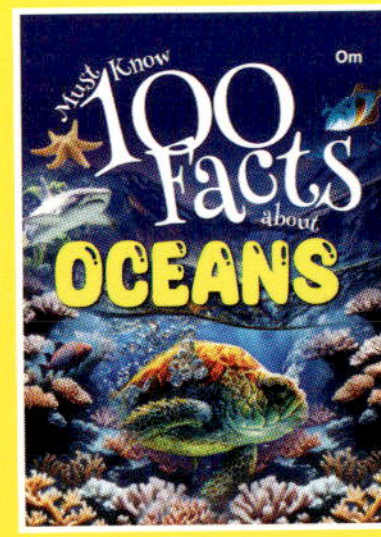

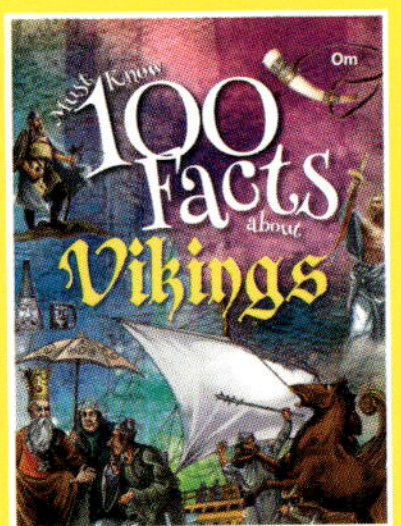

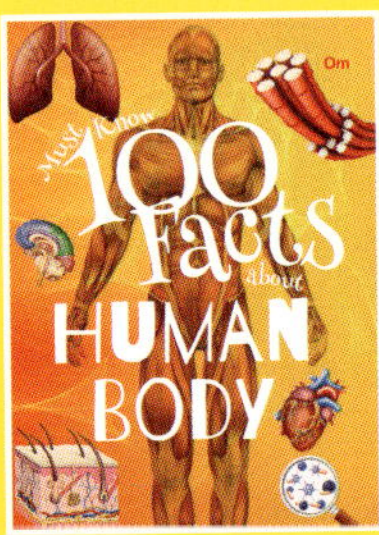

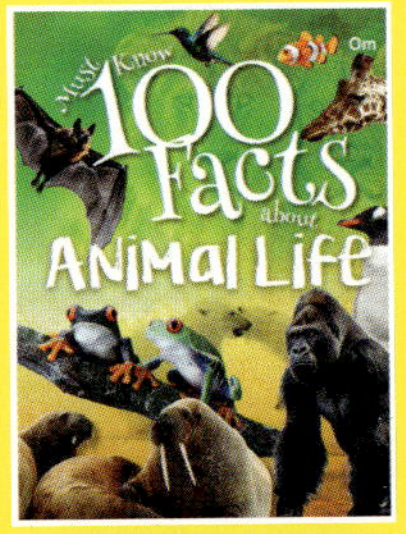

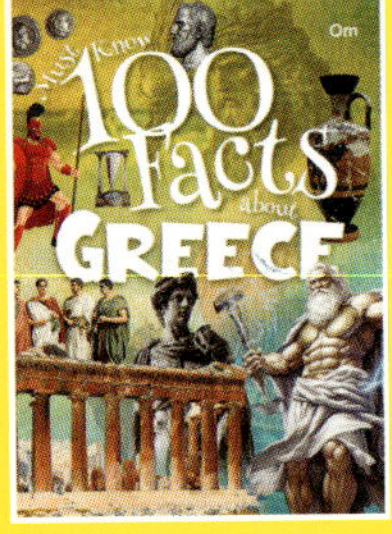

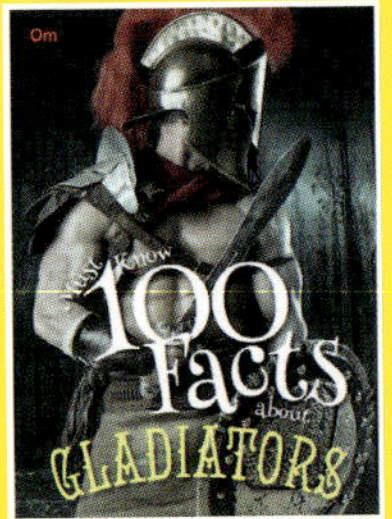

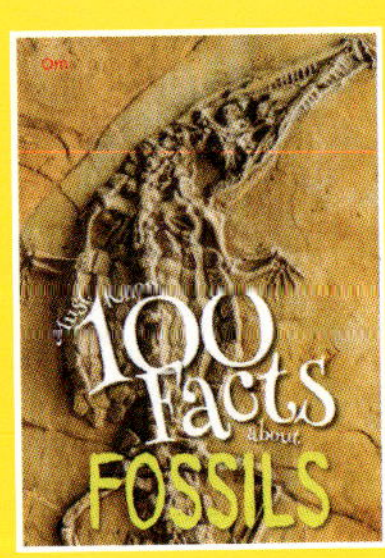

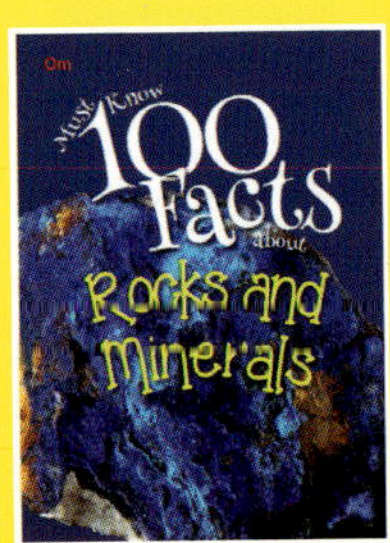